NAKE

Dear Reem,
~~It's~~ It's been a
highlight of my year
getting to know +
working with you!
Enjoy! Ashley

NAKED SALES

HOW DESIGN THINKING
REVEALS CUSTOMER MOTIVES
AND DRIVES REVENUE

ASHLEY WELCH
& JUSTIN JONES

LIONCREST
PUBLISHING

NAKED SALES

*How Design Thinking Reveals Customer
Motives and Drives Revenue*

ISBN   978-1-61961-756-8 *Paperback*

978-1-61961-757-5 *Ebook*

CONTENTS

———

INTRODUCTION

THE $3 MILLION BUS RIDE

When Sachin Rai boarded the Greyhound bus in San Francisco, he had little idea that the trip to Los Angeles would land him a multimillion-dollar sales contract.

Sachin was an experienced account executive at Salesforce, one of the world's largest cloud-computing companies. He was searching for strategies to close deals faster while enjoying his job more. That's when he joined our Somersault Innovation Sell by Design program, where we teach salespeople how to become authentically customer-centric. For Sachin, the noble and logical idea of putting the customer first paled in comparison to the pressure of meeting his numbers. Sound familiar?

When we started working with Sachin, we suggested he choose an account in which he could experience their service *as a customer*. He chose an account he'd been trying hard to sign: Greyhound.

He packed his things, loaded up his curiosity, and set out on an eight-hour learning journey on a California freeway. He would talk to *everyone*, from ticket sellers to baggage handlers to bus drivers to customers. We asked him to pay attention, take notes, shoot pictures, and fully absorb the customer's experience.

The long-term goal, of course, was to sign the bus company as a client. The short-term goal, however, was to conduct deep research so he could understand Greyhound through the eyes of a passenger. If he could teach the C-suite something they didn't know about their customers, they might finally engage.

As he boarded the bus, the first thing he noticed was a frowning, frustrated driver filling out a lengthy report with pencil and paper. "Why did he have to waste time on that, before starting the journey?" Sachin wondered. He asked the driver, who sighed and explained the tedium that is filling out the maintenance details of the requisite service log form. The entire maintenance reporting process was woefully inefficient, and it often resulted in a suboptimal passenger experience, such as inoperable Wi-Fi.

So fascinated was he with what he discovered in his observations southbound that Sachin decided to take the Greyhound-owned BoltBus on the return trip from LA to San Francisco. The BoltBus offered an automated ticketing process. The "automation" was a tablet, but it was so slow the driver used a "hack"—a workaround to bypass company procedure—to speed things up. The hack? You guessed it: he used pencil and paper to record passenger boarding information. When your company's technology is slower than a five-thousand-year-old technique used by the ancient Egyptians, that's probably a red flag.

Sachin didn't discover any of these revealing details about the "automation process" during his initial online research. But because he was willing to immerse himself in the customer experience, he was rewarded with these valuable insights. He then used this information to open doors with Greyhound's lower-level executives. He emailed them and explained he'd taken a long ride on their bus and asked if he could share some feedback he had as a customer.

He received immediate responses from C-suite executives. They were astounded by what he had to say. The problems he described had been invisible to them from their vantage point. In fact, the vice president of digital strategy had never taken an eight-hour ride on her company's bus. Greyhound's COO brought Sachin in to discuss the problems he'd witnessed.

WHAT JUST HAPPENED?

Typically, Sachin would have walked into Greyhound's office with a product to pitch. In fact, before riding to LA, he had already begun designing a driver app solution he later discovered would have been totally irrelevant. He would've struggled to convince a junior-level gatekeeper to send him on to a decision maker. He never would've been in the same elevator as the COO, much less invited into his office.

Instead, Sachin showed the COO pictures he took with Marie, his driver, and he shared her frustrations about the service log form.

The COO was awestruck that Sachin knew what the service log was and was eager to look for solutions. The two sat down to work together on a solution. Eight months later, Sachin and his team were able to build this relationship across multiple channels into a $3 million global deal. It was far beyond what Sachin had hoped for.

Salesforce had initially envisioned a marketing deal, but Sachin's insights led to ideas that included a much larger solution with a customer community app, a bus app, and a support app. Because of his firsthand experience, Sachin was able to explain how these apps would work in concert to benefit customers and drivers, as well as Greyhound's bottom line.

Sachin and Salesforce credit the Greyhound deal to the Sell by Design process.

In this book, we'll delve into the specifics of Sachin's tactics and give you detailed prompts and exercises to put his actions into practice for yourself. The most important element of his success, however, was something that occurred before he ever set foot in a bus depot: his mindset. Sachin succeeded where Salesforce had previously failed because he shifted his perspective from salesperson to customer.

Rather than go into a client meeting armed with the pitch of a salesperson, Sachin literally spoke the language of the company. He understood the service log form, the inefficiencies involved with it, and how these impacted the passenger experience. He had educated himself with the knowledge of internal Greyhound operations with which other salespeople were unfamiliar.

When you begin your sales approach with the intent of understanding the client's issues from their point of view—and their customers' point of view—you position yourself for greater success.

OBJECTIONS

This is a book by salespeople for salespeople, so we can already sniff out a few of your "yeah, but's" from a mile away. Here are a few of our favorites.

- *"I Don't Have Time."* Who has time to bus hundreds of miles and take pictures? Sachin's eight-hour commitment earned him whatever commission he was due, which is compelling enough in itself. We get it, though. It's hard to make time to play the role of customer for every potential client. Fortunately, you don't have to: our Sell by Design principles can be applied in everything you do, whether you have eight hours or five minutes. One of our core principles is the customer-centric mindset. We don't mean just saying that you are customer-centric; we mean living it. It's hard to walk the talk. We know; we're salespeople, too. So, here's our promise: use our approach, and you'll start to ask different kinds of questions that will get you into doors more quickly and take you deeper into conversations with prospects, allowing you to close bigger deals faster.

- *"I only sell B2B."* Whether you work in B2C, like Greyhound, or B2B, like Deloitte, your client has customers. Your task remains the same: focus on the needs, issues, and constraints of *their* customers and understand how to affect your client's bottom line. No matter how complex your client's business, their customers are the one stakeholder around whom everyone can rally. We want to help you and your clients enjoy similar success. We want you to ride their metaphorical bus. In all your research—whether in person, on the phone, or just Googling—whose bus are you on? Is your mindset focused on what you want to pitch, or are you riding your client's bus, asking about their customers' needs?

- *"I've already talked with my client about poor customer satisfaction, and guess what? They don't care!"* Shocker! Not every client is passionate about providing the very best products and experiences for their customers. They may be more motivated by profit. In that case, pay more attention to the experiences of their employees and how they do their work. Are they efficient, or are they coming up with hacks to work around obstacles in their way, like the drivers Sachin met? Chances are, there's a cost associated with those hacks.

Sachin tells us he no longer sells products; he sells solutions. He identifies his clients' problems, offers ideas, then works with them to co-create solutions. "My talk track used to be about the Salesforce product," he says. "Now, it's based on my experience with a customer's product."

This may sound obvious, but we fail to do it consistently as we fall into habitual routines and get distracted in our never-ending race to reach our numbers. It gets really hard not to succumb to what is quickest or easiest or routine.

THE PROMISE OF THIS BOOK

We've hacked sales. We're offering a virtuous cycle of connection, empathy, possibility, and motion. The results you'll experience will be tangible and measurable: more meaningful conversations with clients, increases in pipeline and contracts and fewer calories burned along the way.

In the following chapters, you'll learn:

· How technology is disrupting sales, and how to keep up.
· A proven recipe to drive revenue and add more art to your science of sales.
· A series of tools to uncover more insights about your clients.

- Specific prompts to discover untapped problems.
- How to use insights to get into the C-suite quicker and easier.
- How to use agility to hear fewer noes and inspire bigger yeses.
- How to integrate Sell by Design as a sales manager to reduce pressure on yourself and your team while kicking serious butt.

We've designed this book as a manual for quick and easy guidance. Read it from cover to cover or skip around as appropriate to your situation and interest. Use it as a doorstop if that's useful. Our hope is that you're reading this book because you're usually on the lookout for ways to add to your game. If what follows in these pages aids you in that effort in even a small way, we'll have succeeded.

WILL ANASTAS, FORMER SVP ENTERPRISE SALES, SALESFORCE: "SBD SEPARATED OUR AES FROM ALL OTHERS."

Sell by Design separated our account executives (AEs) from others in the marketplace. Most AEs did web research, flaunted publicly available info, and immediately proposed a solution. Our AEs came in with firsthand knowledge of their clients and their customers, which created an authentic connection and soon led to breakthroughs.

We used to need thirty touchpoints to get a conversation going with new customers. By taking a Sell by Design approach, that number has been reduced to fifteen—a 50-percent reduction in the prospecting process.

Managers can also slow down because once they see reps are having authentic brand experiences, they know they have a higher chance of making a deal. There's less stress and more patience. Reps are no longer missing the big things that matter. Plus, it does not slow down the sales process, once our reps are trained. And it produces tangible business results.

It elevates you from vendor to partner with the customer. You have demonstrated you care about their business, and you've told them things about it that they may not even know. It's far more valuable (and enjoyable) to be a partner than a vendor.

This is the ONLY training we've done that we can directly correlate to increased pipeline and that turned into increased bookings. It was highly measurable and added millions of dollars to the top line.

Sell by Design is fun, different, and a differentiator.

PART 1

SALES, REDESIGNED

Chapter 1

THE WORLD OF SALES IS CHANGING RAPIDLY—ARE YOU PREPARED?

———

We want to start this book with you. The sales professional is at the center of everything we do. Chances are, you're currently doing quite well. Maybe you don't mind putting in the work because the payoffs (autonomy, good money, fast pace, interesting people, among other perks) can be pretty fantastic. And when you're starting out, it can be especially fun. Your products and services are new, as are your customers—there's so much to learn. You hit your number, your number gets bigger, you hit it again. Your customers love you. You're a success. You love sales.

We love it, too. We both started our careers in sales, and we're still selling every day. But we've noticed that despite our experience, it doesn't seem to be getting easier. In fact, it's becoming more difficult for a couple of reasons. First, the world out there is changing faster than any clichéd way we can phrase it. It's truly a case of disrupt or be disrupted. Second, our professional experience can, paradoxically, get in our way.

Let's begin with the rapidly changing environment.

Retail chains are closing stores and signaling that they'll likely go bankrupt. Amazon, which recently announced thousands of new hires and entry into the grocery industry, makes it so easy to purchase items inexpensively that retail margins are eroding. Technology is collapsing the space between customer and designer or manufacturer, disrupting the traditional middlemen: Sears, Macy's, and the like.

This is happening across all industries, even those that are more regulated, such as banking, insurance, and health care. Salespeople need to adjust. Permit us a used-car sales story to illustrate further.

DISRUPTION ILLUSTRATED

CarMax is one of the country's largest car-selling entities. You can do your research online through their service and show up at the dealership with all the information you need. There's no more haggling or reluctantly agreeing to pay for add-ons (what the hell is a "protective undercoating" anyway?). You know exactly what you're getting, as well as the fair-market value.

That's if you even bothered to show up. You might save yourself some hassle and just buy the vehicle online via CarMax, Carsdirect, Carvana, or myriad other sites, eschewing physical stores, salespeople, and their commissions entirely. Technology is collapsing the space between the person who has a need and access to their solution.

To make all of this work seamlessly, client businesses are becoming increasingly complex, and salespeople know it's getting tougher to shine. We have to keep up with digital transformation, artificial intelligence, the cloud, machine learning, and the Internet of Things. Within technology companies, salespeople have an especially hard time even keeping abreast of what their own company is selling. It can be overwhelming.

In the past, salespeople had an informational advantage, which gave us a leg up on the customer. It was easy to walk in, authoritatively overcome objections, and convince people of your correctness. Those days are over.

Customers can Google anything on the spot. They are more knowledgeable and, thus, possess more power, and by the time they meet potential vendors, they're further along in the buying process than ever before. Sales itself is being disrupted. We need innovative ways to add value to our clients.

A second factor making sales more difficult than ever, in contrast to rapidly changing technology, is not external at all: it's our own success. Brace yourself: you could very well be your own worst enemy. Dang!

Remember those sales targets we talked about? Hitting them consistently doesn't make them any smaller. On the contrary, they only get bigger. The number is everything. It keeps you up at night. It determines whether you'll be able to make your next car payment. It directly affects your health and well-being. On some level, you *become* your number.

Hitting that number is just one of the challenges that makes sales so exciting and so rewarding—and so stressful. The goal of reaching the President's Circle is alluring. So you create shortcuts. You cultivate relationships with clients and become more efficient by learning to read them better, developing questions that lead to matchmaking with your products and services. You rely on your favorite products, product combinations, and pitches. You maintain tried-and-true replies to objections to stay in control of the deal. You ink the deal and keep moving. You're good.

And in doing so, you miss really important opportunities.

For as much as our expertise serves us well, the flip side is that it also blinds us to new opportunities that, thanks to the aforementioned rapidly changing business environment, are increasingly harder to identify and more important to long-term success.

Under the pressure to perform, our seemingly successful habits can turn us into revenue drones—we're good at spotting things from a distance, but we're still missing what's important on the ground. As such, we kill the creativity required in a disruptive market. To survive, salespeople need to shift from *experts* to *collaborators*. This means learning to understand customers well enough to codesign solutions for their ever-evolving needs. We're no longer living in a seller-buyer world. Success in this new world is achieved by sitting on the same side of the table.

This can be especially tricky for those of us who specialize in a specific sector or vertical. The more routine your work becomes, the more you could be in trouble. We recently spoke with one of our participants from Hyland Software, who said he had twenty-five different clients in the same industry. They all have similar needs, so he can go in without much research and sell them all the same thing. Most of the industry groups use the same software. Easy peasy.

He's a successful guy, but we pushed him to dig deeper, knowing that his success might be plateauing him. When he did, he discovered he wasn't fully realizing the extent of his opportunity. "I fear," he said, "that if I did a little deeper discovery—like you're teaching—that I could have tripled the size of those deals. There's so much more there."

Is there anything so bittersweet as leaving something on the table after closing a deal?

The reality is, many of us in sales show up overdressed in the habits from our past. We might even be using new technology tools, such as data analytics, for example. If our only interest in these tools, however, is in predicting which customer will buy product X or service Y so that we can save some time in determining our pitch approach, we're falling further behind. Only *human data* can predict the solutions customers will care about. That human connection helps you see through the customer's eyes and talk authentically with an insight that compels action. That's why we're firm believers in stripping away our tried-and-true pitches, our favorite product talk tracks, and our fail-proof list of pain-point questions. Yep, we want you to get naked. We want you to see with fresh eyes what's really there in your clients' customers' experiences.

Despite major advances in sales technology, the oldest one is still the best: our ability to connect with other people. It's one of the few human capabilities that technology can't replace.

HOW CAN SALESPEOPLE KEEP UP?

Yes, the business world is changing at the speed of technology, and yes, your own expertise can be your Achilles' heel, but no, the sky is not falling. If you're successful now, you'll probably continue to be. We're only suggesting that you are capable of more—much more. We want to help you close bigger deals, identify important opportunities for your customers, and continue to succeed by reconnecting with them in an authentic way so that catchphrases such as "customer-centric" and "trusted adviser" aren't just trite buzzwords, they are your modus operandi. The alternative is to mire yourself in the present routine, which is essentially to say, the past.

IS THIS WHERE DESIGN THINKING COMES IN?

In a word, yes: this is where Design Thinking comes in. Design Thinking and sales might sound like unlikely bedfellows, but, in fact, they're star-crossed lovers. Design Thinking—a.k.a. Human-Centered Design, or, if you dig brevity, "Design"—is a creative problem-solving methodology used in the pursuit of innovation. Whether you're innovating a product, service, or experience, you are, by definition, seeking to create something new, something that didn't exist before. That means you can't know at the outset what your solution is going to be. So how do you get there? Well, designers start with the people for whom they're designing: the "users." The user is the person or group of people whose thinking or behavior you hope to influence through your innovative solution. In our case, the user can be our client's employees or, more powerfully, our client's customers. The client's customer is the ultimate end user.

Design Thinking calls for deep connections with the end user. How deep? Deeply deep. So deep that you can empathize with and even anticipate their needs and reactions. You become trusted advisers to the extent you connect with your clients' customers and can share that experience. Clients are more willing to listen and entertain bigger opportunities if they understand how their customers are impacted. There's more credibility on the account executive or sales side; and on the client side, there's more trust and engagement.

As the salesperson representing your company, you're the closest to the client and the end user—your client's customers. You initiate the relationship between your company and potential client, so you have a unique opportunity to help your client make a change. It's *your job* to connect deeply with end users to improve their experience. You can't rely on marketing intel or customer analytics alone; you must generate your own firsthand insights in order to earn adviser status. Design and sales are personal.

And even though your client has access to more information, you can't rely on them to identify the correct or underlying problem or opportunity. You must become fluent in the customer experience wherever it takes place: online, in a store, in a meeting room. You must become a solution designer and "Sell by Design." When you do, you'll strip away all the noise and reveal customer insights powerful enough to compel your client into action and partnership.

WHY WE DO THIS WORK

We love working with salespeople because you're smart, innovative, and demanding. When we work with sales teams, we know we have to pass a hefty sniff test: *Are you worth my precious time and attention? I've got stuff to do, money to make.* We love that challenge, and we've proven the payoff of our approach.

Ashley spent twenty years selling for a boutique leadership development firm. She succeeded at the highest level, which meant her $4 million quota (the largest in the company) increased every year. Despite her success, she left her firm to start Somersault Innovation with Justin, who had also worked in sales and marketing. We were heading leadership and organizational change projects with *Fortune* 500 clients when we stumbled upon Design Thinking. We both saw the potential it had to transform sales and were inspired to make a difference in the lives of our fellow salespeople and their customers.

We're both wired to connect with people, but we bolster that with a "get shit done" approach. We're always looking for hacks and ways to side-step the heavy, process-oriented stuff we too often see; we'd rather provide specific and useful tools that can be easily wielded in the real world.

We don't expect mastery at either sales or design; we merely want to nudge people into new and more profitable territory as quickly as possible so they can see results for themselves and keep moving forward. That's why we're called Somersault Innovation. Try something new. Play around with it to make it work for you. *Somersault*. Take a leap that inspires. And make your work more fun.

Chapter 2

HOW DOES DESIGN THINKING MARRY UP WITH SALES?

———

When we sell, we're trying to solve a client's problem—ideally, with an innovative solution. All too often, when we innovate or problem solve, we are bogged down in matters of feasibility and viability. *Feasibility* involves determining whether a potential solution can be readily integrated into the business—is it feasible to do? *Viability* involves the financial side. Can a new approach sustain or grow our business model and profit targets?

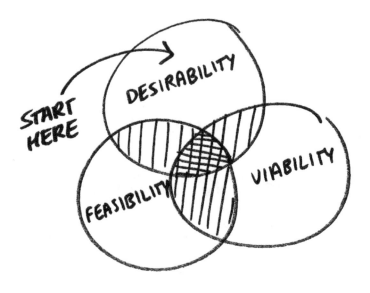

These are very important questions that we ultimately do have to answer, but they ignore something equally, if not more, important: *desirability*. What's important to the people who will use these products/systems/tools/processes/solutions and ultimately create the value necessary to make a profit? Designers believe that while we ultimately must solve for all three of those areas, we should begin with people and go from there. If we don't find a solution people want to sign up for, we're diminishing both the feasibility and viability of our solution in the end.

The process of Design Thinking generally occurs in three main stages: user research, insight generation, and solution experimentation. We'll review these briefly.

USER RESEARCH

As we've said, the primary focus during research is connecting with end users: the people whose thinking or actions you want to influence. It focuses on real, living, breathing people on the ground. Data is important in problem solving, and Design Thinking uncovers the human element within the data.

It's one thing to learn about a ticket-scanning application for a bus driver to efficiently board passengers. It's another thing entirely to witness what happens when a driver tries it for the first time, gets frustrated by its slow operation, feels embarrassed in front of impatient passengers, and worries about a tight schedule. Design starts with and focuses on *people*.

INSIGHT GENERATION

In the second stage, designers use what they have discovered to form insights: interesting points of view based on user research that can lead to new solution ideas. You can't generate innovative solutions without new insight. So designers seek to connect the dots they've uncovered during their research to come up with compelling insights.

These insights usually lead to much bigger questions. When you realize, for example, that a customer experience is heavily correlated to "driver experience," a new question comes to mind: How can we leverage technology to give drivers a seamless experience so that customers are delighted as well?

SOLUTION EXPERIMENTATION

Finally, designers seek to validate their solutions by immediately engaging users for feedback with a very rough approximation of the solution. Rather than fretting over a perfect solution that can be rolled out as-is, they engage the user with a quick prototype or prototypes and enroll the user in iterating the idea into perfection.

This co-creative approach saves time, builds confidence and buy-in for the solution, and ensures the user gets something that really works for them in the end.

THE HISTORY OF DESIGN THINKING
(YOU KNOW YOU'RE INTERESTED)

Design Thinking was initially used for product design as early as the 1960s. In the next decade, it started to be codified and formalized and was adopted by architects and city planners. In the 1980s, Stanford University was largely credited with using the methodology for creativity in general. In the 1990s, the product-design consulting firm IDEO became well known for using Design Thinking as their overarching methodology with their clients. Since the turn of the century, Design Thinking has boomed and is starting to be used to create all manner of experiences, services, and processes—from medical devices to sustainable food systems. Several colleges and universities have begun offering a "Design MBA." We're here to bring it specifically to sales. No DMBA required.

MATCHMAKING: DESIGN THINKING + SALES

We like to keep things simple, so in creating the framework for Sell by Design, we've kept the three-phase process of Design Thinking (user research, insight generation, and solution experimentation) and overlaid the most basic sales cycle.

Phase 1 is *discovery*, in which we learn about the client, their business, and their customers.

Phase 2 is—surprise!—still *insight*, in which we collate

the interesting things we've learned from discovery into points of view that can add value to our clients.

Finally, there's Phase 3, which we like to call *accelerate* because it's all about co-creating a solution with your customer to drive deal velocity and move quickly to close.

As you can see in our model, each of the three phases is brought alive by a specific mindset. We'll also give you specific tools for each phase, but it's really these mindsets that make all the difference in terms of what you can accomplish with your client and how well you'll leverage the tools. First, allow us a matchmaking analogy to illustrate why this marriage works so well.

Have you ever been on a date with someone who spent nearly the entire time talking about themselves? Maybe they were halfway decent about feigning interest in you with a few choice questions. But after you answered, you saw that their questions were all a ruse intended to set them up to tell yet another *amazing* story about themselves. *Check, please!*

Brace yourself—that's exactly what salespeople sound and look like to many clients: we walk in with a big smile, chat for a bit, then start asking questions related to the product or service we have in mind for them already. Sure, it's obvious we're there to make a deal and sell something. There's no harm and certainly no shame in that. It's honest, professional work. But why settle for a professional relationship when both sides could be swept away? We've all had that great experience of connecting in a genuine way with a client and putting together an inspiring deal. It's fun. And it often leads to bigger opportunities, either immediately or over time. Why can't we do that *every* time?

That's where Design can help. You don't have to be a "creative type" to use these innovation tools. In our experience, we're all creative types. To the extent we already have a solution in mind, it's hard to be creative: we're like the proverbial dog with a bone. What we lack is an easier approach to client challenges and opportunities, which would otherwise allow for more creativity.

Design helps us keep our thinking open. Rather than narrowing in and converging on a known solution for a known problem, Design encourages us to look deeper and broader to diverge into other interesting areas that could lead to a more creative approach.

That's not always easy to do, especially when you can see dollar signs on the table, and your manager just asked about your numbers during the morning meeting. An account executive (AE) working with a large Canadian bank recently took this leap of faith. His client told him they already knew the solution they wanted; they just needed a short product demonstration for members of the leadership team, then they could sign the deal. Cue the slot-machine sound effects!

The AE walked excitedly into that meeting with eight senior leaders—empty-handed.

"Where's the demo?" they asked.

"I haven't brought one," he confessed. "And I'm sorry to disappoint you, but I began to worry that I don't know enough about your business and your customers to demonstrate what we can really do that will help you. If you'll give me an hour today, I promise I'll make it worth your wait."

(A cricket chirps somewhere in the room.)

"*Ahem*. Well, what would you like to know?"

He proceeded to learn far more than he previously understood about their business, and the leadership team actually enjoyed the conversation. They thanked him at its conclusion. And, yes, you guessed it, the additional insight they provided led the AE to think of a more robust solution idea, which he was subsequently able to demonstrate. *Bam!*

The Holy Grail in discovery—for either Design or sales—is the same: it's deeply understanding your client and *their* customers. Keep in mind, you're at least two steps removed from the end user when you first connect with your prospect. Do you really understand what your client's customer cares about? Have you physically put yourself in the end user's shoes, like Sachin did with Greyhound? Have you at least interviewed or researched them closely enough to identify with their experience? What and how you research can have a big payoff.

Discovery in this sense doesn't necessarily mean more time on your part. More than anything else, it's a mindset shift. It's delaying our focus on a specific solution and spending more time up front learning about our client, their customers, and their business so that we can spend less time closing the deal later. The counterintuitive move is to set any talk of solution off to the side so that you can gain genuine insight into the client's business. The payoff for this is that once you *do* get to the solution (yes, you'll get there), the customer has had a hand in creating it and they're ready to move faster to implement. The net effects? Shorter overall sales cycle times coupled with bigger deals.

We tested this shorter sales-cycle theory with a cold-calling sales team at Salesforce. We liked this team because they were true pavement pounders—dialers and smilers who worked only on new accounts. They called themselves "hunters." They knew that the average number of "touches" (a call, email, or other point of contact) necessary to get an initial meeting averaged out to thirty.

After working with us for three months, that average dropped by 50 percent, to fifteen touches, and they were pulling down some major deals. What did they change? They spent more time up front learning about their clients and, importantly, *their* customers.

You'll find the insights you derive from your research range from the somewhat mundane to the shockingly insightful. Regardless of where your insights fall on the spectrum, they're incredibly valuable. The *only* requirement is that you learn something interesting you didn't know before. For example, upon visiting a Bay Area hospital client, an AE was struck by the importance of their value of "human kindness." He saw this stated in posters in nearly every hallway, on their mission statement, and in many impromptu hugs he saw care providers give to patients. This became insightful, as it contradicted the medical systems he watched both patients and care providers use. Those systems were antiquated, clearly frustrating, and anything but kind. The juxtaposition of their value for kindness and the patient and care provider experience sparked the motivation for change.

When you get to that magical acceleration part of the conversation—the solution ideas you'd like the client to consider—this becomes a bidirectional conversation: a dialogue. You don't have to worry so much about presenting a thorough, buttoned-up solution. Instead, offer several low-fi options. Ask the client to help shape their favorite. If your solutions are anchored in the insights that matter to the client, you're golden.

An AE shared his thinking with us about the solution he wanted to share with the SVP of sales operations at IBM's Watson Health. He had carefully thought through all the ways they could address each of the specific issues their discovery work had identified. At the same time, he knew the SVP was looking for inspiration. So we encouraged him to come up with three different options and not worry about perfecting any particular one of them:

1. His original 'known solutions for known problems' approach.
2. Additional applications that could be added for more value.
3. A whopper option with some funky artificial intelligence woven in.

All three were rough sketches, not the usually pretty PowerPoint deck. She loved it! She was so inspired that she took ownership for championing the cause internally to win support. The AE didn't need a fully baked pitch; he needed to paint just enough of a picture based on shared insight to inspire action.

Design Thinking is about resolving the realest, biggest

problem, with an open mind rather than assuming you know the right answer. It allows you to design a rewarding solution for both parties as part of a two-directional, co-creative conversation. It's not a one-sided Power-Point presentation.

MORE ART THAN SCIENCE

In many ways, Sell by Design will feel more like the *art* rather than the science of sales, which is why it's so different from other sales methodologies. Rather than giving you scripted approaches to move a client through your sales cycle, we'll focus on enabling the right mindset and then leveraging simple, useful tools.

We'll show you how to hack the art of selling. We take the best of the Design methodology used by the most successful companies in the world—Airbnb, Apple, Deloitte, Facebook, GE, Google, IBM, Johnson & Johnson, Microsoft, Procter & Gamble, Salesforce, and SAP—and put it in your hands to solve big problems with your clients.

PART 2

SELLING BY DESIGN

Chapter 3

PHASE 1: DISCOVERY

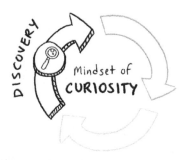

In this chapter on discovery, we'll spend some time determining the quality of your curiosity, a necessary mindset. We'll provide four specific discovery tools you can use to deepen the quality of information you can elicit, as well as the degree of connection you'll enjoy with your client and their customers. Finally, we'll share a few thoughts about discovery strategy—namely, where to focus your attention for maximum insight.

The Sell by Design process starts with *discovery*, and the driving force that empowers your discovery is a mindset of curiosity. Of the three phases of Sell by Design, this phase is probably the most important because it sets everything else up for success, and that success hinges entirely on the quality of your curiosity.

AN EXAMPLE OF KICK-ASS DISCOVERY

Brianna Layton had been out of college three years. Her sales training at Salesforce gave her a list of questions to help her find opportunities and focus the customer on Salesforce products.

Given that we're creatures of habit, she would ask the same basic questions regardless of whom she was talking to. Her brain eventually turned off, and she stopped listening deeply, meaning that she was at risk of missing the root of the issue, moving to solutioning before the customer was done exploring their issues thoroughly.

We asked Bri to find an account in which Salesforce wanted to expand the relationship. She chose a large greeting card company. The company's digital transformation officer said the company was having trouble connecting with Millennials and that they were worried about becoming the "Kodak of cards."

In order to connect with their customers, Bri visited stores and watched and interacted with company employees. She asked employees to show her how they interacted with and kept track of customers, with whom she also spoke.

Then, she went online, submitted her info, downloaded a company app, and documented response times and details with screenshots.

Along the way, she gathered several different insights about gaps between experiences Millennials would value and how the company was engaging them. She realized she'd have to give the company's executives some tough love. So, at the start of her meeting with a room of executives, she began with a personal story. She shared how she used to make greeting cards as a child and how she would always put this company's logo on the back of her cards because it meant her cards were special. She then explained the disconnect she had experienced between this brand promise and her own experience as a Millennial customer. She shared high and low points in her experience, how frustrating the app was, and how slow responses were. Then, she shared a few ideas about how Salesforce could help them keep their promise with Millennials and invited the executive team to debate the ideas. Before she could take her seat, the execs stopped her: "Please stay right there." They had questions for her, lots of questions.

Her discovery prompted a genuine conversation with these executives, one that was all about *them* and the experience of their customers. Her enthusiasm and caring were so clear, and every pain she mentioned highlighted a clear opportunity for a solution.

Bri and her team signed the client to a seven-figure deal.

Prior to meeting with us, Bri had considered getting out of sales. For her, it had become cold and transactional. Sell by Design made sales personal and enjoyable. By focusing her discovery on real people and understanding both the employee *and* the customer experience, she became fluent in issues that mattered to them. She could speak their language and engage them to help her craft the best solution.

We can appreciate that you might think you're already curious enough as it regards your clients. Based on our experience working with hundreds of successful sales professionals like you, you're very likely not. There are two reasons we lack a sufficient level of curiosity, not only as salespeople but also as *people* in general. The first concerns our human nature; the second is that we rarely learn *how* to be curious.

THE MINDSET OF CURIOSITY

Most of us in sales lead with expertise and a "closing energy" rather than a mindset of curiosity. We know our company's products and services inside and out, and we're masterful at quickly linking a client's needs to our solutions. This is the wellspring of our credibility. Our employers see us as successful sales professionals because we can predictably deliver revenue right on schedule. It's a self-perpetuating cycle that gains momentum as we become more experienced. And it's a trap.

It's a trap for all of us in sales because it leads to mind-numbing monotony, even burnout. It's a trap for our clients because even though they might be happy with our quick solutions, we haven't helped them see other possibilities that could help them accomplish even more. It's also a trap for our employers because we're either leaving opportunity on the table (also a bummer for us in terms of lost commission), or we're inviting the competition to come in and go further, or—most likely—both.

We want to emphasize how normal this is from a human standpoint. It's not that we're all assholes. Everyone wants to be seen as competent, and we want to help our clients Most of us do sincerely care about solving our client's problems. But we get in our own way. We lose our edge. We start to sound like an automated phone tree.

Think about the last time you called, say, your credit card company or your cell phone service provider and got the voice-activated prompt promising, "You can say whatever you want, and I'll connect you." Sounds great, but if you don't articulately use one of the predetermined prompts the system is programmed to recognize, good luck. You end up saying, "*representative, representative, REPRESENTATIVE!*" until you finally get through to a real person.

Too often, our sales experience has reduced us to automated phone trees. There's little authentic connection and interaction. Harvard researcher Amy Cuddy talks about this limited connection in her book *Presence*.[1] She found the first thing people do in most professional interactions

---

1   Cuddy, Amy. *Presence: Bringing Your Boldest Self to Your Biggest Challenges.* Little, Brown and Co, 2015.

is *try to project competence (expertise)*. We're eager to show what we know and what we can do, and we believe this establishes our credibility.

Of course, competence is important. If you're an idiot, who would want to spend time with you? Interestingly, Cuddy's findings show that before people seek to understand your competence, they seek warmth. *Can I trust you? Are you real? Are you someone I can connect with?* By rushing to display our expertise and competence first, we downplay and sometimes miss our chance for authentic connection. And that's extremely costly in sales.

In Sell by Design, we talk about embarking on discovery with a beginner's mindset. We even talk about becoming vulnerable with our clients, even if it feels awkward. We focus more on noticing what we don't yet understand, rather than seeking to confirm what we've seen and done in the past. That's where the magic lives.

A Salesforce AE was struggling to gain traction at a small, neighborhood coffee company called Starbucks. He had done his usual discovery work: website and online searches, 10-Ks, annual reports, and industry analyses. He's a sharp guy, and he knew he could provide several solutions that would help the company. But he was having no luck getting in the C-suite.

He took our advice to heart, to learn something new and stay curious about his customer—to approach the company like a beginner. He decided simply to visit a Starbucks in the evening, when business would be slower, and talk to a store manager. No agenda. No pitch. He asked her about the joys and difficulties of her job.

After building rapport, he asked one of our favorite questions: "What's the bane of your existence?" Without hesitation, she pulled out a massive "milk binder" and explained how difficult it is to manage the store's extensive milk offerings, which included numerous varieties, myriad expiration dates, and specific temperature requirements. We all think of Starbucks as being in the coffee business. Turns out they're also in the *milk* business.

Next, he emailed the executive vice president (EVP) of operations to say that he understood the milk binder needed some innovation. He said exactly nothing about Salesforce products. The EVP wrote back immediately, cc'd another executive, and said, "Absolutely! Could you please talk to this guy?"

It sounds simple, and yet it can be difficult to do. Our mental habits get in the way.

The name for this mental habit is *convergent thinking*. Most problem solvers in business, which is nearly everyone but especially includes salespeople, are consummate convergent thinkers. We love to solve problems and close as quickly as possible. That means inserting our product/solution in at the first opportunity because we can then move on to the next one, en route to hitting our numbers. ABC: Always Be Closing.

Design Thinking, however, encourages *divergent thinking*—the opposite. The idea is to think as broadly as possible in several directions. Learn as much as you can. Once you've discovered the biggest opportunities, *then* converge to the biggest, most mutually beneficial solution.

When you remove the conversation's limits, what you lose in certainty, you gain in possibility. Deal size is limited by conversation scope—why not allow for bigger ones?

As we've discussed, we typically enter a conversation with the assumption that we already know the problem, so we generate a solution based on those assumptions. For example, we worked with a pharmaceutical company that sells an acclaimed oncology product, but their sales numbers and market share were dropping. After holding strategy meetings, they concluded, once again, that their drug's clinical data was superior, so the numbers should speak for themselves. All they had to do, they thought, was republish and redistribute their data more in the marketplace.

They did so, but numbers continued to decline. Then, we taught them a Design approach. Instead of assuming oncologists would care about data, we had them ask why they weren't prescribing the drug. They also asked the oncologists questions they normally wouldn't have considered: about their work, their patients, the best and worst parts of their day—connecting to them as people and understanding their world.

One surprise they uncovered through divergent questioning was that even after decades of working in oncology, doctors still struggled to give patients bad news. While the company's product was superior, it required patients to take a biomarker test beforehand, and then they'd have to wait several weeks before learning whether they were a good candidate for the drug or not. While other drugs may not have been as effective, they had the advantage of being prescribed immediately, and it felt better to the oncologist (and the patient) to offer a quick solution. So they did.

Once they explored more aspects of their customers' experiences, everything changed. They started focusing on how to help oncologists have more productive conversations with patients about care options, and the numbers began to climb again.

We can't preach this enough: *enter every interaction with the assumption that you don't understand the problem.* Start with curiosity, and get to know your client. Conventional wisdom is built on guesswork, and you don't find out that your assumptions were wrong until it's too late—until your well-intentioned idea is underperforming or failing, and you realize you didn't understand the problem or your client.

Design Thinking converts you from being a problem *solver*—like every other salesperson in the field—into being a problem *finder*. If you completely understand the bigger problem, you can design the optimal solution.

HOW TO BE REALLY CURIOUS IN YOUR DISCOVERY

Given our habits of expertise and convergence and the limiting impact these have on our ability to engage productively in problem solving, you'd think there would be an equally developed body of research on how to become curious. You'd be wrong.

However, designers—because they purposefully jump

into the unknown and seek new perspectives that lead to innovative solutions—have figured out ways to magnify curiosity. They've found ways to see the uncommon in the everyday by supercharging their capacity for curiosity. We can, therefore, borrow from Design in order to get better at noticing and discussing interesting things with our clients.

Having worked with hundreds of sales professionals, we've found it's easier to get—and remain—curious to the extent we practice noticing **four specific Design Thinking prompts** in the course of discovery. As we do this, it's astonishing how quickly we become expert observers. These prompts can be readily found both in new accounts, as well as in existing accounts we're seeking to grow. And these prompts are *EVERYWHERE*—just waiting for us to call them out. They're a powerful antidote to our habitual mindsets; they help us fight the gravitational pull of converging on a solution by expanding our focus and our conversation with the client. The more we start to notice, the more we see, and this leads to bigger, more authentic conversations. Here are those four prompts: surprises, hacks, passion, and inconsistencies.

SURPRISES

As we engage with a client, there are an endless number

of unexpected, surprising things that inevitably arise. Our tendency is to sweep these under the rug, to move on and maintain deal velocity. But these little surprises represent important opportunities for us to pause, comment on our surprise, and ask the client some questions.

An AE from a large technology firm in Chicago entered a carpet store, and the employee showed her how they place orders. The employee wrote the order down on paper, then walked the order down to another part of the building to get the carpet cut. The paper-based process surprised the AE, so she asked the store manager whether they ever had problems with the order getting lost during the transfer. Yep. The manager opened (in "ta-da" fashion) a door to a closet filled with miscut carpet. Sharing her surprise led to an authentic moment of connection with the store manager and to an unexpected opportunity.

HACKS

You'll remember that a *hack* is a creative means of improving a system, product, service, or whatever. A Greyhound driver who bypasses the handheld scanning device for boarding in favor of a faster, albeit manual, checklist is hacking the boarding process. A sales professional scanning this book for quick tips is hacking the reading experience.

We're all hackers, and we hack to make our world better. Do you have a ribbon or special tag on your suitcase handle to make it easier to identify at airports? That's a hack. Your suitcase didn't come that way. The power of a hack is that it's evidence of an unmet need—a need you as a sales professional may have a solution for. Another interesting thing about hacks is that once you've created one, you're less able to see it as such. Your hack becomes your new normal. Your clients may no longer see their hacks. When you see a hack in your client's business, investigate. Ask questions about why the hack was created.

PASSION

Practice noticing passion—what do your customers genuinely have strong feelings about? It's easy to downplay emotion in client interactions. We want to act professionally and this often means rationally. Decision making, however, isn't an entirely rational process. Feelings, whether they be of frustration, enthusiasm, or anything else, are the number-one indicator of what's important to people. The extent to which we can tap into these feelings is the extent to which we discover motivation for change and momentum. That's what our AE did with Starbucks: by tapping into a source of frustration for the store manager and her employees, he discovered the milk binder. Moo.

INCONSISTENCIES

Finally, people and organizations are full of inconsistencies and contradictions. They say one thing is important, but there are many other indications to the contrary.

Remember that greeting card company with a clear strategy to engage Millennials? Many of the experiences they offered customers contradicted their strategy. Elevating this gap so that decision makers could see it led to a seven-figure deal.

These four simple prompts will shift you from being an expert to being a detective capable of finding underlying problems while building great client rapport. Give it a try the next time you're working on client discovery. Start with the assumption that you will learn something interesting you didn't know before, and then practice noticing these prompts and see what happens as a result.

MATT WOODHAMS, ACCOUNT EXECUTIVE, SALESFORCE: "IN SALES, WE ARE OFTEN SELFISH BY DESIGN"

Before Sell by Design, everything was "me focused," because that's what sales teaches.

I call a customer and enter their life, pitching them *my* product, because *I* want them to buy it, and *I* make money if they do. Then, *I* ask them for more time because *I* didn't get my full pitch/demo in, and that's needed for the process of selling them *my* product. Then, *I* take more of their time to get decision makers to talk to *me*. Finally, *I* ask the customer for money in exchange for *my* product they may not have known about before *my* unsolicited call.

Whether the customer was having a good or bad day before my call, my call wasn't a part of their day. They didn't choose me. I'm entering *their* life to try and separate them from their company's money.

Yes, companies offer value to customers—otherwise they wouldn't exist.

But Sell by Design flipped my script. Now, I look at *everything* from another person's point of view.

The call needs to provide value and context—what does it mean for the customer and their business? Otherwise, my disrupting their day isn't worthwhile, and I'm just being a jerk.

I pay attention to frustration now. Too often, we downplay emotion, but emotion reveals frustration, and behind frustration are unmet needs and solutions waiting to be created. Emotions are also what allow you to land ideas. Don't just say, "Look, this is going to save you money and time." Connect with their frustration. "We could save you and your customers a lot of grief and make them love you in a way that they just don't right now."

Recently, I went to a large outdoor retailer to do discovery. I posed as a customer and suggested I was ready to buy and had a budget. The rep captured my information on a sticky note, and then never called to follow up! When I shared this story with the retailer's executive, he cringed and quickly calculated what they were losing on large vehicle sales, based on the percentage of leads they knew came through the door...and it was millions of dollars. "Don't let leads fall through the cracks" became the subject of our conversation—something meaningful and real to the executive.

When Ricky Gervais created *The Office*, he didn't just Google "office life." He went to work in an office, so he understood firsthand what it's like. Similarly, if we don't do in-person discovery or be a customer of our customer, we don't have much to go on except assumptions and our selfish-by-design pitch rather than the actual real life "what it's like" to be their customer.

DISCOVERY TOOLS

The four prompts are designed to develop your curiosity muscles. They clue you in to powerful elements of your interactions with clients and their customers. These work best to the extent that you can engage with people. In addition to your online research, 10-Ks, quarterly and annual reports, press releases, and executive bios, you need to understand how your client creates value. Do they sell products and services in a coffee shop or carpet store, online or on a bus, B2C or B2B?

Understand what that looks and feels like for employees of your client and, especially, for their customers. Here are some discovery tools to help you leverage your curiosity and deepen your understanding. The more curious you are, the more powerfully these tools will serve you.

FLY ON THE WALL

When you're in one of your client's stores or in their offices, observe what's going on without intervening, just like a fly on the wall. Watch for curiosity prompts as you see how people engage with each other, how they interact with products, services, or even their environment. What do people care about, and are those needs being served effectively and efficiently?

The next time you're waiting for someone, put down your phone. Don't check your email. Pay attention to everything going on around you. You'll notice things you've never seen before.

We often send students out to visit nearby paint stores to watch the action. Paint stores are interesting because for many of us, choosing the right paint color is an important decision. But paint stores don't seem to understand this. You'll notice people staring wide-eyed at a wall full of color options. Will it be "orange sherbet" or "tangerine"? It's overwhelming. And you can tell how difficult it is just by watching. Very few paint stores are effective at helping customers make decisions.

BE THE CUSTOMER

Become a customer of your client. Whether that means applying for a loan or buying a custom-designed T-shirt—engage in the experience of being the end user.

We worked with a sales executive who was selling his house and buying a new one. He worked with the same real estate company for both sides of the transaction and noticed some interesting things. He was later able to share his experience in a business meeting from a customer point of view, because, as it happened, he was also prospecting this real estate company in his own sales process.

One frustration he had was that the "For Sale" sign stayed up weeks after he had signed the contract and moved in. People kept knocking on his door asking to see his new house. The client cringed. They knew it was a problem but hadn't been able to fix it, and it gave the sales executive a way in. This was not a massive issue, nor was it an awe-inspiring insight. But it was important to the client, and it led to a larger, more meaningful conversation. It also revealed to the sales executive the power of being a customer of your client as part of the sales process, as it transforms the conversation.

SHOW ME

Whenever you can go beyond simply talking about something to actually *seeing* it, take advantage of that opportunity. If you simply take your client's or their customer's word for their experience, you risk missing out on a wealth of opportunity. It could be the difference between a carpet store manager telling you they handle customer orders flawlessly, or seeing them take manually written orders down the hallway to the island of misfit cuts.

Whenever someone mentions a process or tool they use to do their work or accomplish a task, ask them to *show* it to you. Have them walk you through what they do, step by step, while you ask questions, either in person or via screen- or video-sharing.

Someone might *tell* you they have an excellent reporting tool with great functionality. Ask them to show it to you. Maybe it's just an Excel spreadsheet. Unless you ask them to show you, you'll never know. They may have a hack with which they're more than comfortable.

When people from different contexts share information

about their experiences, it's hard to know what details to share and what to leave out. We're so used to our status quo that we don't know which details others might find interesting.

Show me is a way to create common context and break through a great deal of assumptions on both sides of the conversation.

DEEP-DIVE INTERVIEW

We've saved the most frequently used discovery tool for last. Interviewing is often the most efficient method for gathering information about clients and their customers. It's especially effective if you're not able to meet with people in person, as you can still discuss their needs and experiences. The trick is finding a way to meaningfully engage in interviews that are rich in the details you need in order to do great discovery. In effect, you're using conversation to approximate *being the customer or show me.*

The best way to do that is to have the person paint vivid images for you with specific stories. In everyday conversation, we operate on the surface by simplifying our experiences through generalizations that aren't always accurate. This graphic depicts the flow of a deep-dive interview.

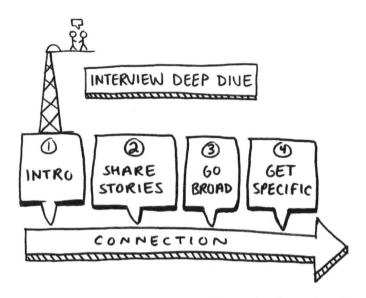

In many respects, the flow of a deep-dive interview is not so different from the typical discovery interview we might conduct, except for two things: first, you'll build more rapport through your curiosity, and second, you'll ask the interviewee to share far more detail via stories than they are accustomed to sharing. This takes some careful framing as you set up the conversation.

INTRO

The beginning of a deep-dive interview is important. We want to build rapport, orient the interviewee to the outcomes we're interested in, give them a sense of how the conversation will play out, and enroll them to participate fully with us. And we want to do this so well that it will be easy for them to share something amazing that we didn't know!

Everyone has their own style of rapport building. The amount of time we spend building rapport in the interview often depends on how well we know the interviewee. In addition to the typical name-role-tenure professional jabber, we like to include something personal about ourselves—that we have kids, where we live, what we did last weekend. We typically start by introducing ourselves as a courtesy, because we're usually the ones asking for the call, and in doing so, we model how we'd like them to respond.

Second, we typically shift to the context and purpose of the call, and we phrase this in terms of what we hope to learn and why we think that's important: "I'd like to ask you some questions about how you process customer loans because I know your customers care about how quickly they get an answer."

Next, we try to set expectations in terms of how the conversation will flow. We let them know we're going to ask them to give us very specific examples so that we can see the world through their eyes. It's important to do this because people aren't used to thinking in terms of specific examples. They're going to want to generalize with you, and you're not going to let them. Providing this heads-up won't stop them from generalizing, but it does give you permission to press them to be more specific later on. You may say something like, "I don't want to assume that I understand your loan process, so I'm going to ask you to share some specific examples—while protecting any sensitive customer information—so that I really do understand how it works. Is that all right?"

Finally, give the interviewee a sense of control in the conversation. If you want them to participate fully, it has to be a conversation they co-own with you. This could be as simple as asking what questions they have before you begin, or asking if there was anything else they were hoping to get from the discussion.

SHARE STORIES

Hopefully, this is where you'll spend most of your time during the interview. You might start with some softball questions to get the ball rolling, but before long, you want the interviewee to pull you into their world. Stories are the very best way to do this. You win in your deep-dive interview to the extent that your interviewee gets lost in their stories.

Because people aren't used to accessing specific examples like this, in addition to giving them a heads-up in the setup, we need to help them by using prompts. Ask people variations of *last*, *first*, *best*, and *worst*. For example:

- When was the *last* time you had this problem?
- When was the *first* time you noticed this issue surfacing?
- What's the *best* instance of when this process works for you and your customers?
- What's the bane of your existence (*worst* thing) in your role?

The power of these prompts is that they help you to encourage people to search their memories for specific instances to share with you. These specific instances will give you rich data; however, it will take effort on their part to consider them, and, possibly, some time as well. The biggest mistake we see salespeople make after asking a great prompting question using *last-first-best-worst* is filling the silence with another question or rephrasing the question. Just shut up. Don't be afraid of the uncomfortable silence. Let them think; let them speak.

Once the interviewee identifies a story and begins to share it, use brief *what* and *how* questions to move along the horizon of their experiences so that you don't miss anything: "What happened before that or next?" "How did they complete a particular step?" Very importantly, ask plenty of *why* questions to make sure you understand the motivations of the people involved. Never assume you know these. Be on the lookout for passion! When you hear the tone or pace of their voice change, or, if in person, you see how much they care about something, you *must* ask them about it: "It seems as though this step causes you and your team some friction; why is that so important to the entire process here?"

Warning: don't make the mistake of assuming that just because you've encouraged the interviewee to share a specific story, you can hit cruise control and lean back in your seat. Great storytelling is a two-person dance. The storyteller needs a great listener to bring their story into the light of day. This is where your supercharged curiosity converts an average discovery session into an amazing conversation. Sharing a personal story takes effort, and it's revealing, which can make people feel vulnerable. They need to know you're in it with them so that they'll feel safe enough to share the juicy details you need to understand if you're going to do great discovery.

Yes, this includes the subtle, barely verbal "*Mmm hmm*" and "*Oh?*" But true authenticity also requires that we comment on surprising or unexpected elements, noticing the tone of their voice change because they're sharing something very personal or important, which might identify it as a passion, as we discussed earlier.

When we comment on these details, we paraphrase what they've said that piqued our curiosity or surprised us so they know we're really listening. If you both get lost in the story, you're really rocking it. One of the best measures of your curiosity is the extent to which you enjoy the interview. It should be fun! You should have learned something new, and that just feels good.

We worked with an AE based in Sydney, Australia, and she did such an excellent job of eliciting stories, demonstrating authentic curiosity, and participating fully with her interviewee that he dropped a bombshell neither of them expected. They were discussing how the client managed their home security products in the warehouse and on technician vans when he suddenly shared recent examples of how employees had been stealing company property and selling it online. It was a big and embarrassing revelation that surprised the interviewee a little when he shared it. For the AE, it reflected the depth of trust and rapport she had created, as well as a key motivation the client had for change and for finding a partner he could trust.

GO BROAD

Before moving to the conclusion of the interview, ask your interviewee an aspirational question: "What do you think the ideal solution should be?" If you've done a great job in eliciting powerful stories, it's likely that many new ideas will have occurred to both of you. Make sure you understand what they think an amazing solution could be, and why.

GET SPECIFIC

During the close, it's so important to acknowledge your interviewee for the gift of insight they've given you. Like any thank-you, the more specific you are, the more meaningful it will be. Don't just thank them for their *time*. Ugh. Please! Be a real person. Don't be weird. Tell them what you most enjoyed about the conversation; tell them what you learned that truly inspired or interested you. It could possibly open yet another door: "Well, if that was interesting to you, let me introduce you to so-and-so because they're trying to figure that out right now."

Finally, share your next step—whom you want to talk with next, where you'll go with this information, what additional requests you might have of the interviewee, and so on.

I'M CURIOUS, GOT MY TOOLS, WHERE DO I FOCUS? SOME THOUGHTS ON DISCOVERY STRATEGY

Design Thinking channels its curiosity toward the end user. The end user is the individual, group, or groups whose thinking and/or behavior your solution will impact, and a deep understanding of these people is paramount. For our purposes, this means we need to understand our client's customers: who they are, what they care about, and what their experiences are like.

It's also important for us to understand the experiences and beliefs of the client's employees—the people in our client organization closest to their customers. It's about getting in their heads. That means getting beyond the default habit of talking about our own products and services. Connecting with real people—your clients, their employees, and their customers—will help you get outside of your product or service box and see more opportunity than you otherwise would. These people are the best qualified to help us see more.

We're not suggesting you cast aside the other forms of research you typically conduct. Company reports, industry publications, and executive bios all provide important context and can provide direction and insight, but your client's ultimate business value happens at the points of contact they have with their customers. The better you understand what those contacts look and feel like—whether digital or physical—the more differentiated a business partner you'll be.

This means visiting client stores, talking with employees and customers, visiting websites, and trying out client apps; calling customer service lines to talk about a product you want to purchase or have purchased. And so on and so forth.

If you want or need to save time, think of ways you can pressure test your client's system. You want to look for the above touchpoints or moments of interaction, but you can cut some corners by identifying more extreme instances of when and where these interactions take place. In other words, you *could* just be an average customer and look for average interactions—making a typical purchase using a typical method. Or you could consider extreme examples that might give you even more insight more quickly. For example, what's it like to buy their most expensive or involved product or service? And then, what if you had a complaint or needed to return the product? An AE recently had "an issue" with a barbecue grill he purchased (he actually did have an issue in this case). As he pursued the customer complaint process, his service agent had difficulty finding his receipt and simply refunded him for the entire grill! What?

How do they handle small, customized orders as opposed to large-scale demands? Ask your *best-worst* questions. What do their happiest, most loyal employees and customers say about them? How about when people are pissed off? How do they handle that? Extreme scenarios can save you time by getting you to interesting insights faster.

WHAT ABOUT B2B CLIENTS?

Doing discovery for B2B (business-to-business) clients isn't as easy as walking into a coffee shop. What if you're working with an insurance company? Or a Big 5 consulting firm? Or a manufacturing conglomerate?

Every client has a customer, and the more complicated their business model, the more likely there will be an expansive web of customers reaching out to one or more groups of end consumers. Your task is the same, but you're going to need to be more thoughtful in your approach. How many customer perspectives can you connect with across your client's network and value chain? The more customer dots you can connect, the more you'll provide a daisy chain of value and insight.

Here are some ideas to spark your imagination for connecting with employees and customers of your B2B clients:

- Who do you know who works at the company or who buys from them? Check your LinkedIn network. Talk with your colleagues and friends; who knows somebody who works there? An AE was flummoxed about how to break into a health-care provider when he remembered that his wife, a nurse, had friends who worked there.
- Are any of your other clients customers of this particular B2B client? What's their experience like? Could they introduce you to their contacts? We recently had an AE creatively set up a feedback session where his client's customers could share what it was like to do business with them.
- What does Glassdoor.com reveal about the employee experience of your client? What about customer reviews sites or industry award reports? Are they constantly hiring certain types of positions? What if you applied for a job?
- Does your own employer do business with your client? One account manager was struggling with access to one of the largest accounting firms until she realized her employer was their customer! Bingo.

While you may need to do some more creative thinking with your B2B clients, your objective is still the same: identify and experience what your client and their customers care about. You'll always find real people trying to solve real problems.

NOW WHAT?

You've captured a lot of fish with your net, but what do you do with them? How do you serve them up?

Insight generation is next, and we'll introduce interesting ways to connect dots to spark conversations with customers, which will lead to more inspiring solutions and bigger deals. We told you at the beginning of this chapter that discovery plays a disproportionately important role in the entire Sell by Design cycle. Accordingly, having done a thorough job here, you'll find that subsequent chapters—and the application of them—will go more quickly.

Chapter 4

PHASE 2: INSIGHT

This chapter, like insights themselves, is a short pause we want to insert between your discovery and any solution pitching you'll do when you accelerate. Many of us don't reflect enough on our discovery before we shift into full-on sell mode. Even as we conduct our discovery, we're salivating over all the things we can sell. While it's great to feel inspired about a prospective deal, we're suggesting you rein in your multimillion-dollar pitch a tad longer and think about insights—it could be the difference between no deal and something bigger than you could have imagined on your own.

As Bri's example illustrates, the benefit of kick-ass discovery was identifying compelling insights she could share with her clients. She wasn't making a laundry list of all the things her client was doing wrong or of all the Salesforce products they could be using. She noticed several disconnects between experiences the greeting card company created for its employees and customers, and its stated strategy of connecting with Millennials. The *insight* she engaged them with was about how an important customer category was experiencing their brand. She didn't talk about Salesforce at all. And she ended up sealing a very big deal.

Let's talk about the mindset for this phase, what an insight is, then how to create and share them with your clients.

A MINDSET OF EMPATHY

In the discovery phase, our mindset was one of total curiosity—the beginner's mindset. This helps us get the clearest view into whatever is going on with our client and their customers. When we shift to insight, the question we're trying to answer is "Why are these things we've discovered happening?" The mindset that best helps us answer these *why* questions is one of empathy. Empathy helps us understand the viewpoints of the various stakeholders we've encountered in our discovery. It helps us see the world from their perspective, to walk in their shoes. Curiosity can help you discover the milk binder, but empathy helps you understand why it's important to the employee who complains about it, as well as why it's important to the company that has become accustomed to using such a tool.

Empathetic salespeople behave as if they work for the client. The best salespeople we know *get* their clients because they dive so deeply. They speak their language, use their abbreviations, sometimes even adopt mannerisms and other cultural nuances when they interact with their client.

It can be especially hard to be empathetic as a salesperson. Empathy necessitates opening yourself up to people. You need to be—here's the "V" word again—vulnerable. That's often more difficult because sales requires a tough skin. No matter how good you are, you're getting the door slammed in your face regularly. Yet you've got to be hoofing it all the time—activity is king, it drives sales, so you better not stop. To the extent we've toughened this steely, rejection-proof veneer, we leave less space for empathy.

That's why we love Dan Pink's clever reframing of ABC from "Always Be Closing" to "Attunement, Buoyancy, and Clarity." In his book *To Sell Is Human* he, too, advocates close connection: attunement with clients, staying buoyant so that rejection doesn't stop you, and a focus on clear insights that can create value.[2]

There's a fair amount of focus in sales today on becoming a trusted adviser. We believe that Selling by Design—doing deep discovery with great curiosity and empathizing with your clients to generate meaningful insights—is a guaranteed path to trusted adviser-ville. What could be more trust building than someone who not only understands your business and your obstacles but also empathizes with what you're trying to accomplish and why?

Empathy earns you the right to tell people the truth, even when it might be hard to hear.

SO WHAT *IS* AN INSIGHT?

It's a good question, and there isn't an easy answer. After all, there are insights and then there are *INSIGHTS*. We define an insight as a hunch about your client that you find meaningful and that could offer competitive advantage

2   Pink, Daniel. *To Sell is Human: The Surprising Truth About Moving Others.* Riverhead Books, 2012.

to your client. Why a *hunch*? We use this word to remind ourselves that while we may be super excited about something we feel is insightful, it's possible our client couldn't care less. Remember the example we shared with you earlier about the real estate company's fossilized yard signs? Calling an insight a hunch reminds us to hold our insights with a lighter grip. That way, we're less likely to white-knuckle our profound conclusions and use them to convince our clients: "No, you really *should* care about my amazing insight!" It's less about being right and more about demonstrating our authentic interest.

Insights also offer value to the extent they inspire us. As we connect dots along the journey of our discovery, our growing insights keep us intrigued and motivated. They can even point us in new directions as we connect more dots. Ideally, our insights inspire our customers by revealing a novel point of view to them, even if it's considering something they hadn't reviewed for a while and elevating its priority. Typically, the power of an insight correlates directly to its degree of "non-obviousness." The less predictable your insight, the more likely it will be considered valuable by your client.

Again, bear in mind the word "hunch." You might be dead wrong. You don't have to feel pressure to come up with amazing insights; you might come up with something relatively small that still connects you to the customer and invites them to open up and advance the conversation. The insight doesn't necessarily get you the deal, but it does get you connection and moves you forward together. Its value is in authentically engaging with the customer, which will then make them more likely to reveal even more to you.

It may feel unnatural to pause your selling so that you can share your hunches before you discuss solutions. Nevertheless, it creates a competitive advantage for both you and your client. Pause and reflect on all that great discovery work you did. What are the most interesting things you know? What's the story that's forming, and what is its importance to the client and their customers? If you jump to a solution, you risk missing out on a larger opportunity—or worse, the solution you've formulated is dead wrong. The pause you take to formulate insights could save you the wasted time of crafting the wrong solution or a solution no one cares about but you.

THE CHALLENGER SALE METHODOLOGY

Several of the sales teams we've worked with have also been trained in the Challenger Sale methodology. As with Sell by Design, the Challenger Sale also advocates the use of insights. There are some important differences in our terminology. However, we also want to emphasize how well our version of "insight" stacks up with Challenger Sale's version. They work great together.

In Challenger Sale, the salesperson provides industry insights and seeks to educate the client on a larger point of view. You use insights to provoke and teach. You attempt to show the client something they're missing or could be doing better.

Sell by Design advocates on-the-ground insights that come from the client's employees and customers. We're not talking about insight in the big-data way. Those are secondhand insights. We favor insights that are firsthand, which become *your* story rather than your attempt to tell someone else's story. It's powerful due to its immediacy, and even more so when combined with relevant secondary industry insights.

Telling a story about the coffee-growing industry, or evolving role of the CIO is important, but it's not as real and connective as a first-person story about the milk binder and the frustrated look on that manager's face. Once you've connected, you can talk about numbers. Big-data, industry-level insight is valuable, but it won't help you connect as well with the people you're talking to.

HOW ARE INSIGHTS DERIVED?

Often, insights occur organically while conducting discovery. We notice a manual order entry process, and we instantly have a hunch about unintended problems with order errors. There are also deliberate steps to deepen insights about a client and their customers. We're going to discuss two of these: Customer Journey Maps and Jobs to Be Done.

CUSTOMER JOURNEY MAPS

Customer Journey Maps, as the name implies, portrays the experiences of customers with your client across a variety of touchpoints over time. But its real value—either to you or to a client with whom you might share your Journey Map—is not just the existence or sequence of touchpoints; it's all about the customer's *experiences* of those touchpoints. Journey Maps help us visualize the larger customer experience by revealing each step of the way—from walking in the door of our local Starbucks to taking the first sip of our latte—along with patterns of interaction and experience. They reveal high points and points of friction—both of which might be capitalized on by your client.

SAMPLE CUSTOMER JOURNEY

· GETTING CAFFEINATED ·

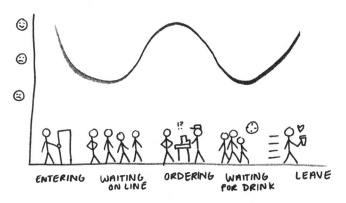

ENTERING · WAITING ON LINE · ORDERING · WAITING FOR DRINK · LEAVE

Your Journey Map can range from the highly unsophisticated, such as our example here, to the highly detailed, and there are plenty of templates to be had, courtesy of Google.

Generally, you plot the customer touchpoints from left to right along an x axis. Then, for each of those touchpoints, digital or physical, you plot customer experience on the y axis, a range of positive experiences increasing in positive intensity above the x axis, and increasingly negative experiences below.

This tool's value is that it can help you (and possibly your client if you share it) quickly determine moments of delight and moments of cringe. It could even help reveal patterns that are invisible when examined piecemeal. We've seen Journey Maps used very effectively to deepen discovery with clients for even more insight—where a moment of friction on the map sparks even deeper conversations about the underlying operations that cause it.

JOBS TO BE DONE

Tony Ulwich developed Jobs to Be Done,[3] and it was popularized by with Clayton Christensen from Harvard Business School.[4] It started as a marketing tool and has since gravitated and morphed to the world of Design.

The tool follows the famous quotation from Theodore Levitt, an economist from Harvard Business School: "People don't want a quarter-inch drill. They want a quarter-inch hole." In other words, it's easy to generalize about what people want and put it in terms of what we're used to providing. In this example, a drill manufacturer sees customers as wanting their products. But that entirely misses what their customers actually want. Jobs to Be Done helps us get below the surface and connect with underlying motivations more effectively.

---

3   Ulwich, Tony. "Turn Customer Input Into Innovation." *Harvard Business Review*, January, 2002.

4   Christensen, Clayton, Scott Cook and Taddy Hall, "Marketing Malpractice: The Cause and the Cure." *Harvard Business Review*, Dec 2005.

Here's how you use the tool: whatever thing you've noticed—an experience, tool, product, service, and so forth—can be thought of as a job the customer is hiring it to do in order to accomplish something. If you've noticed a hack, it's the converse—they're firing something because it wasn't doing the job they wanted. What job does the thing serve? What do customers want? What's their motivation? What's the outcome they're seeking? Why is that important to them? Keep in mind that jobs aren't solely task or function related. As our graphic suggests, we hire things to satisfy emotional needs as well—for ourselves and for others.

Christensen illustrates this with a story about a fast-food chain looking to increase milkshake sales. They followed the typical strategy of gathering focus groups and analyzing their thoughts on varying milkshake qualities: flavor, chunkiness, and thickness. They gathered what they thought was great data, then revamped their milkshake formula. They were going to sell *so many* milkshakes that they'd probably need more cash registers.

Sales didn't budge.

Afterward, they applied Jobs to Be Done. They did first-hand discovery, watching customers buy milkshakes, looking for the *jobs that milkshakes served*. The surprising thing they noticed was that half of all milkshake sales occurred before 8:00 a.m., and buyers drank them in their car during long morning commutes.

They asked customers why they were buying milkshakes at breakfast time. They phrased it: "For what purpose—what *job*—are you buying milkshakes at 8:00 a.m.?" Eventually, they came to understand that customers wanted three jobs done: something that would be filling, last the length of the commute, and wouldn't make a mess. A nice combination of emotional and tactical needs.

In Sachin's Greyhound example, the job of the service log

form was twofold: provide a pleasant and safe experience for the customer and provide drivers with a simple-to-use tool to capture and communicate issues. The service log form needed to be fired because it accomplished neither job effectively.

Use the Jobs to Be Done framework to go from discovery to identification of a specific gap, inefficiency, or opportunity—and to connect the dots. The model will help you reveal underlying motivations. Note that all of these dimensions may not be relevant, so explore what is useful. Questions to consider include:

1. What's the job the service-tool-product meant to do?
2. What functional and/or emotional needs are being met by this job?
3. For emotional needs, are these personal, social, or both?

ATTRIBUTES VERSUS MOTIVATION

These two insight tools are powerful because they provide a glimpse beneath the level of attributes and get at human motivation. It's one thing to talk about the tartness of cherry flavor in a milkshake or all the database fields that might be included on a service log form report, but what ultimately matters are the human motivations at play. What are people trying to do, and why is it important to them? This makes our insights more practical and powerful.

Salespeople typically focus on the attributes of the product being sold and the extent to which they match the client's environment. It's far more effective to focus on your customer's motivation: whatever underlies and explains their thoughts and actions. Heidi Grant Halvorson, PhD, social psychologist, speaker, and author of *No One Understands You and What to Do about It*, explained that if you can connect to people's motivation, they'll spend twice as much money as they would have because they value it more.[5]

It all goes back to *desirability*. Sachin was able to connect far more dots by focusing on passenger and driver motivations than he would have had he focused solely on tool functionalities. His insights from that experience were far more accessible and compelling to the executive team.

HOW CAN I BEST SHARE MY INSIGHTS?

Empathy helps you derive insights, but it's equally important to *deliver* an insight with empathy. Empathetically sharing insights transcends the typical buyer-seller

---

5   Halvorson, Ph.D, Grant. *No One Understands You And What To Do About It.* Harvard Business Review Press, 2015.

dynamic. You're no longer a salesperson trying to impose and convince; you're a team member helping frame and achieve a mutual goal. That's also competitive advantage for you as one of any number of potential vendors because other salespeople often don't share this mindset.

As we've mentioned before, when you're empathetic, it's easier to provide people critical feedback. Your insights could reveal some embarrassing gaps. If you're not empathetic, people will likely get defensive. Empathy allows you to discuss issues in a way your client can engage and tackle them with you.

Depending on how much discovery work you've done, you may derive several insights. How do you determine which hunches you should share with your client or which ones you'll want to lead with in your next conversation? You'll recall we defined a strong insight as something that's both interesting to you and potentially valuable to your client's business. If you have a lot of potential insights and are trying to decide where to focus, create a simple four-box model using these criteria.

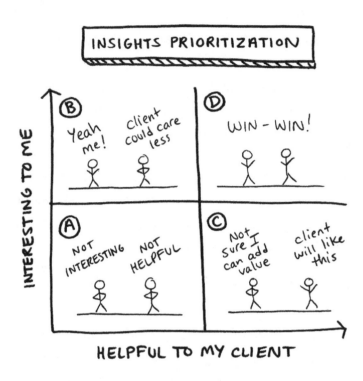

Once you've plotted your insights, the easy decision will be to drop anything in A for the time being and lead with whatever's in D. If you have nothing in D, it might be an impetus for more discovery work.

This simple framework can help prioritize which hunches might be most inspiring to the client.

INSIGHTS MAKE ALL THE DIFFERENCE

Once you've confirmed your hunches, and hopefully

discovered new ones, *then* co-create a solution. Get the customer involved. When you make conclusions on your own, you risk being wrong, and that's a HUGE risk. When you confirm hunches and co-create with your customer, you *can't* be wrong.

Next, we'll examine the co-creative approach in the final phase, which will accelerate your solutions.

Chapter 5

PHASE 3: ACCELERATION

———

You've done great discovery, and you've shared insights to build engagement. Because you understand your client and their customer, you can capitalize on that momentum to close a bigger deal. It's time to accelerate toward a solution that will help your client; perhaps even moving your client faster and further than they might have thought they could go.

A MINDSET OF AGILITY

The mindset in discovery was *curiosity*. For insight, it was *empathy*. The mindset in the accelerate phase is *agility*.

It's good to feel genuine excitement about your solution idea—you should. If you're not excited about it, no one else will be. That excitement can be a double-edged sword, however. If you're too enamored with your idea, it may be hard to hear anything from your client that's south of outright enthusiasm. That's a high-risk proposition: all or nothing. You're betting everything that your solution is strong enough to get a yes, but if you get a no, or even a maybe, you're done.

If you're still empathizing with your client, you recognize that the easiest answer is always no. Even if the client is unhappy with the current state of affairs, *no* means they don't have to expend any additional thought or energy than they did before you waltzed into the room.

Better, then, to be *agile* and prepare a handful of solutions, so that you aren't wed to any particular one. You may distinguish your favorite and explain your reasoning, but you'll be less stuck on any single path forward and better able to hear your client's pro and con reactions to each.

Ask which parts they agree with and which they don't. Build

on the former; scrap the latter. This decreases the likelihood of an outright no, instead engaging the client with the positives and negatives of the options you're presenting.

The objective of pitching a solution that can be accelerated isn't necessarily to negotiate the biggest deal possible (although that's cool when it happens). Instead, help the client feel confident about finding an approach to improving their business. Ideally, your solutions won't be fully baked when you present them. They should be finished enough that the client gets the gist of it. Final agreements, however, will come faster to the extent the client works *with* you to put on the finishing touches. It demonstrates that you're building their confidence and their shared ownership in the solution.

BE AGILE, LIKE AN IMPROV ACTOR

When it's time for you to pitch, the pressure's on. This is your time to shine. So you craft the perfect PowerPoint deck and rehearse in front of the mirror. Stop!

The more committed you are to the outcome or flow of the meeting—just as you've imagined it—the more mechanical (read: dorky) you're going to come across.

Instead, share responsibility for the best outcome with

your client. Assume they'll play a part in shaping the final answer—and tell them this up front. Think of it in terms of attending an improv show. Good improv actors have the skill of listening *deeply* to what the other players and the audience offer, and then they build on it in the moment. It's much more engaging and real than putting on a rehearsed performance in which everyone else is reduced to a passive observer.

The world of improv has some great principles that apply to sales. Legendary British director Keith Johnstone coaches his actors to, "Listen to be changed by what is said." In other words, don't listen with the intention of reloading or finding the perfect retort to an objection. Comprehend what is spoken in the meeting. Find a way to build on what's been offered.

In fact, that's another improv guideline: everything that happens is a gift. See it that way. Yes, that means even an objection. If a client objects, they're trying to tell you what's important to them. Your job is to figure that out. Use the improv phrase "Yes, *and*..." When a client vomits all over your best idea, think to yourself, "Yes, and you're saving us all a great deal of grief by not wasting our time on something that won't work for you. Let's move toward what *will* work."

Don't worry about winning or losing the deal. Hold your ideas lightly. See how the client responds. The goal isn't to ink the first iteration of the deal; it's to find common ground, then co-create the real solution together.

ONE MORE AGILITY ABILITY

Here's another common question we get from sales professionals: "What if the customer doesn't want you to do any discovery but instead just wants an immediate demo or quote and won't take no for an answer?"

Don't be discouraged; there are many reasons this could be the case. Maybe the customer doesn't trust you yet, or maybe they've already done plenty of research, and they're certain of their problem or opportunity and the solution. You're not going to make fast friends disagreeing. You can, however, make a quick deal that gives you both what you need. Agree to give them what they want (the demo, the proposal, etc.), but in return, make clear that you'd like a dialogue about your ideas to learn what resonates and what misses with the client and why.

In so doing, you're turning your pitch into discovery. The Sell by Design process is the same as any sales process: it's cyclical. It almost doesn't matter where you start. What matters is how skillfully you move through the cycles—the mindsets you exhibit as you do so.

WHAT EXACTLY IS CO-CREATION?

Co-created solutions are participative. The idea is to keep the client engaged because it's a partnership. Even after a deal is inked, the relationship will remain. It's not a zero-sum game in which one side wins at the expense of the other. The goal is identifying and crafting a solution that excites both sides, which requires coming up with it together.

With that in mind, the term "pitch" no longer reflects the salesperson's role. Our friend Stuart Paap, who owns Pitch DNA, taught us his concept of the "anti-pitch." He's a successful improv actor who now coaches entrepreneurs and business leaders on their pitches. His work is analogous to ours in that he helps his clients win support for whatever new idea they're seeking to bring to market, obtain funding, and advance their cause.

A classic pitch is one-directional: *I have this solution, let me tell you all about it, and this is the part where you say yes.* As we've mentioned, this is a high-risk proposition. It increases the risk of getting a big fat NO. Plus, even if they do like your idea, there's a good chance something even bigger was possible that you'll have missed if all you were after was yes or no.

An *anti-pitch* means the answer isn't a binary yes or no. It's two-directional. The client is engaged and *co-creating*—if they don't like something, you suggest a better option. Both sides are simply looking for the best way forward, whether it was your first suggestion or something totally unexpected.

You aren't selling; you're *solving*.

The client shouldn't feel convinced, persuaded, or—obviously—sold. They should see their fingerprints all over the deal.

This approach eases the pressure. You don't need to put the perfect case together, just something you can work with. Instead of pitching them what you think will get a yes, you look to excite them to co-create value and allow them to shape it with you.

GIVE YOUR CLIENT OPTIONS

One way to ease clients' concerns is by giving them options. Stuart offers his clients a spectrum. He starts with a minimal option: minimal cost, minimal risk, minimal change—but minimal or lesser impact. Then, he offers a stronger solution in the middle of higher value, and finally, an exceptional option. The last one is a big investment but has the biggest payoff. By framing it that way, the middle one seems like a less intimidating option, but he still provides the option of the massive solution with which to inspire. We also shared a previous example in which an account executive (AE) offered known solutions to known problems, the same known solutions plus some additional value-added options he believed would help, and a third crazy-transformational option to inspire new thinking and ideas.

Don't be afraid to offer a massive solution, but also offer smaller versions of it. Or, offer the massive option as a menu. You can always start small and close the big deal later. You want the big deal, of course, but increasing a client's confidence in their purchase is more important. Confidence leads to trust and bigger deals. This is a long-term game. That's co-creating. That's the anti-pitch.

THE TOOLS: HOW TO ACCELERATE TO A MASSIVE DEAL

We often think of ourselves as closers, but in reality, we're change agents. If you're presented with a change, "no" is the default answer, and it's easy to say it.

Neurologically, we're wired for predictability, consistency, status quo. People may know their current solutions suck but also feel crushed by the imagined weight of having to change. At least their current situation is certain. They know how to tolerate it. It's the obligation of the sales-person to help clients envision the potential that change represents—to see themselves clearly and confidently in that possible future.

There are two ways to help a client embrace a bigger solution: First, excite them about an idea by helping them connect with it emotionally. Second, simplify the solution by helping them see a clear pathway to it.

The goal is to anchor the client in their future desired state—to help them feel it emotionally and see it visually. If they're enamored enough that they can see themselves in that future, change shifts from scary to approachable, even exciting.

We'll look first at the emotional and motivational aspect. The best way to convey and invite emotion and connection is through storytelling.

STORYTELLING

Recall that we wanted you to gather information through story in your deep-dive interviews? We're essentially using stories for the same—though inverse—purpose here. Storytelling is a way to convey complex information in a way that your customer can connect with it.

Remember Bri? She used several stories to great effect. First, she told her own personal story about how she associated with the greeting card company's brand. It was a powerful story about how, even as a child, she knew what they represented. Then, she shared several customer stories. She had the ability to talk about real customers and about her own experiences as such—what she experienced and, especially, how that felt as a Millennial.

This firsthand, emotional form of storytelling—with real-life details—is incredibly powerful in getting clients' attention. It can be far more effective than abstract concepts or numbers, which while important to include, aren't as engaging or memorable and don't help sell a vision of possibility.

Stories have been a powerful part of human experience since, well, forever. Recent research explains what we know about this intuitively. MRIs display a surge in brain activity when we're engaged with story. We retain more detailed information and are more likely to take action. Dopamine, oxytocin, and other chemicals flow more freely in our brains, enhancing memory and increasing feelings of cooperation.

Salespeople invariably default to use cases when presenting solutions. It's a form of storytelling. It's saying,

"Here's a company similar to yours, and here's what they did. So, you can do it, too." This anecdotal evidence is effective, certainly, but misses the mark to the extent it doesn't include three key narrative components your stories *must* have:

- Character-driven
- Emotional
- First-person

These three ingredients make stories compelling, connective, and memorable. They're also generally missing from use cases, which make them cardboard-dry. If you're sharing a third-person use case with your client, you're asking for low engagement.

Suppose you're anti-pitching to executives at Gillette, and your idea is to help them better educate their customers on the specific type of razor they should use. There's likely an extensive library of secondary research, industry insights, and fabulous use cases about the joys of customer education in consumer product goods that we could point to.

Instead, we'd like you to meet Anne. We checked out a local CVS to get a firsthand look at how customers interact with razor displays. It was a slow day for razors, as it turns out, and we weren't having much luck with customers to watch or talk to.

Then, we met Anne.

Anne had seen us hanging around aisle 5 and came over to see if we needed help. To our surprise (and good luck), she was the store manager and had been for twelve years. We explained the purpose of our research. She was immediately enthusiastic.

She said she'd noticed the majority of razor shoppers were women buying for someone else. She'd see them standing around, just like us. They weren't involved in research, of course, but they were obviously overwhelmed by the vast selection. Furthermore, if the store was busy and Anne couldn't get to them to offer help, she'd typically see these women leave the aisle empty-handed.

Anne had several ideas for making razor shopping more intuitive, as well as ways to educate the customer...

A few things about this story we'd like to point out:

- *Brevity*. The story can be told in less than one minute. Storytelling doesn't require regaling a client with every detail of the entire discovery journey or covering every insight that's been pieced together.

- *Character-driven.* Anne's the hero of our story, and we want to share just enough information about her to bring her to life: how long she's worked there and so on.
- *Emotional.* We include the visceral aspects of the experience—our *surprise* at her tenure, her *enthusiasm*, and that shoppers felt *overwhelmed*. Everyone can identify with these feelings from our own experiences.
- *First-person.* We were there. We met Anne. We know her. We heard what she said. It's easy to tell when someone's telling a first-person story—and when they're not. If you're going to rely on a use case, at minimum, reach out to people who made that sale and ask for details. Press for information about the specific people involved and what they were experiencing as they worked through that solution. This will enrich your use case.

To be sure, our anti-pitch could be strengthened with facts and figures about possible investment costs and returns on that investment. We're not focused on that here because in our experience, this isn't what's missing in these meetings. What's missing are stories that help the client connect. We like using stories to help the client connect both with the current state, such as our story about Anne, as well as the utopic future state that will result from a co-created solution. We might even retell the same story, with Anne, once our solution's in play: She never visits aisle 5 because customers easily determine which razor they need on their own. And it's a Gillette.

SKETCHING

There's a good reason PowerPoint is the dominant presentation tool. Pictures and graphs simplify complex information. They make ideas digestible and accessible. That's important because most of our thought capacity is consumed by visual processing. Memory, in particular, is highly visual. That's why stories are so helpful; they help us imagine things.

We don't love PowerPoint pitches, though, for a couple of reasons. First, most pitch decks are swamped with My Company/My Product slides. While they're usually beautiful and painstakingly produced by the marketing and graphic teams, they also make us want to throw up in our mouths a little bit because they're all about your company rather than the client.

The other big problem with those PowerPoint decks is that visually speaking, they're finished and perfect. That means they're less engaging. When the slideshow starts, watch the energy level in the room drop like a thermometer in the freezer. People disconnect from each other as their attention and energy shifts to the inanimate projection wall. You might as well just pump sleeping gas into the room.

We recommend sketching as a more powerful and compelling visual tool you can add to your repertoire. Like the anti-pitch, sketching is connective and collaborative. Much of its beauty lies in its imperfection and the fact that it's being created in the moment. Real-time sketching is riveting. Animated educational videos have figured this out, providing narration over sped-up sketching, and creating an entertaining form of information sharing.

The quality of the drawing doesn't matter a bit. There's no art degree required. Simply sketch *enough* of an abstraction that the audience stays engaged. This is "whiteboarding," and while some companies are more comfortable with it than others, anyone—everyone—can do it.

Dan Roam launched a consulting practice and has written a book series called *The Back of the Napkin*.[6] He asserts that everyone is a more-than-capable sketcher. If you can draw five basic shapes—circle, line, triangle, blob, and rectangle—you're capable of representing any idea you wish to convey.

6 Room, Dan. *The Back of the Napkin*. The Penguin Group, 2008.

We can go even further in lowering the bar for entry. Consider this work of art—worth many millions of dollars—sketched by Marc Benioff, CEO of Salesforce, and Angela Ahrendts, then-CEO of Burberry.

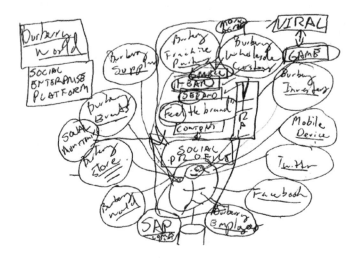

The handwriting is god-awful. The words are barely legible. On its face, it's a terrible drawing. It doesn't matter. The drawing resonated and led to a deal because he sketched it *with* Angela about how their companies could work together.

A PowerPoint may have been more aesthetically pleasing and less abstract, but it also would have been less connective. During that conversation, they co-created and sketched a solution that would not only transform Burberry's connection to its customers but would also lead to the creation of a new retail platform that Salesforce could offer other clients in the retail vertical.

Bring markers to your meetings and start drawing. Invite your client to sketch with you. If they take the marker out of your hand and add a detail you hadn't considered, you've struck pay dirt.

THE "AS-IS VERSUS COULD-BE" TECHNIQUE

Wait, what do I draw? The simplest way to sketch is to draw two scenes: one in the current world, one in your customer's desired future state.

It's essential to include people in your sketches. Stick figures are more than sufficient; they're fabulous. Make sure you show—you guessed it—emotion. Are people smiling, confused, angry, or unhappy in their current state? Show their transformation as a result of your solution.

Stick figures and sketching work because you're explaining and creating them together, in real time. Your client was there with you and can explain exactly what the faces and symbols mean. Your PowerPoint may be twice as beautiful but not half as connective or productive.

In sales, ugly co-creations trump polished works of art.

JENNIFER FORTUNE, DIRECTOR, GLOBAL SALES ENABLEMENT, HYLAND SOFTWARE: "NOTHING HAS BEEN AS STICKY AS SELL BY DESIGN"

We never tell salespeople to just connect, human to human. In the first session, Somersault told people to just connect and listen. Forget the agenda, and don't force people forward in the sales process. It was eye-opening and refreshing to take a step back—to just be human, connect, and relate.

Sketching was my favorite tool because it allowed reps to keep their connection while moving forward in a meeting. Once you're in a meeting and a PowerPoint goes up, there's no collaboration, and you lose the connection.

Sketching allows the customer to collaborate—to draw a new, better version or add or subtract something. Give them the pen.

Salespeople know they should be more human and customer-centric, but do they know how? This approach gives them a tool kit and a practice so that connecting with your customers is unavoidable. That's because it guarantees connections, which opens up untapped opportunity.

There is only one thing that hasn't changed in sales: people buy from people they like. Connecting with people is a superpower. People need to know you care about them and their business, or they won't make a deal with you.

WHAT HAPPENS IF YOU DO THIS RIGHT?

Anti-pitch well and the customer will have a greater sense of ownership in the solution. If they're coming up with the deal, how can they say no? Your relationship gets deeper, competition-proof, and more likely to lead to future deals.

It's a cyclical process because trusted relationships are timeless. Acceleration leads back to discovery for another possible deal. Every step is designed to move you forward, but there is no end. Good discovery leads to interesting insights, which can help you accelerate toward solutions. That leads to even more discovery, more insights, and bigger solutions.

We separate the three phases to distinguish the three mindsets, but our model is nonlinear. You're never *done* with discovery, insight, or acceleration. Even when you're accelerating, you're still doing discovery and gathering insight. You're always building this perpetual motion to move your client forward and, yes, make your number.

Sell by Design is designed to feed on itself. For the client, it builds the motivation and momentum for change. For the salesperson, it keeps you interested, fresh, happy, and engaged—and keeps giving you more opportunities for future deals. We hope it brings you renewed inspiration for your work and even more success in your future.

Chapter 6

MANAGING SALES BY DESIGN

———

Wallace Holland is a regional vice president for Salesforce. He has a team of salespeople who report to him. He holds weekly check-in calls to see what's going on in accounts and get the forecast.

Like most managers, he used to drill down on numbers: "We need to close by Friday. How close are you to $50,000?" Now, he leads by asking them for stories about their customers: "What creative approaches are you using to get close to them? What's something new you've learned?"

Of course, he still asks about numbers. But he starts by asking for stories because that helps drill in the mindset that *the clients' needs come first*, and the numbers will follow. By fixating on the number, the client gets diminished.

Wallace's new approach is to track these qualitative answers just like typical metrics. On one account, an AE mock applies for jobs and reads Glassdoor reviews. For a hotel company, they read TripAdvisor reviews and plan a trip to the company's Las Vegas hotel, where they'll join the players' club to check out the customer experience. They read online gaming forums to figure out which casinos are best and why.

These are Sell by Design approaches.

Previously, Wallace didn't cover these details in forecast meetings, but after implementing our methods, he has become a firm believer because he's seen results.

Wallace sent us his spreadsheet—it was as simple as adding one extra field; one extra qualitative metric to capture the creative discovery methods of his account executives. It doesn't replace revenue and deal stage; it's a supplement.

WHAT DOES SELL BY DESIGN
MEAN FOR MANAGERS?
STOP PLAYING THE FORECAST GAME

There's a game being played: the forecast game. It's what keeps salespeople internally focused. Managers are under pressure, too, so they constantly hound employees: "Where are you with this account? What's the deal size? How soon is this going to close?"

All too often, this is the primary nature of conversations between salespeople and managers, and it forces salespeople to get *creative*, euphemistically speaking. They hide deals they're not confident about because they don't want to be hounded if a deal falls through. If the news is *too* good, your pipeline number is likely to rise, adding more pressure. Better to underpromise and overdeliver.

Such games are a waste of energy. Account executives are incentivized to hide their goings-on, and managers are pressured to hound them anyway.

There's reason for this, of course. Businesses must mitigate risk. They want to be confident that their pipeline and revenue forecasts are accurate. It may make sense, but it misses the opportunity to have any kind of conversation regarding what salespeople are learning about their clients and their client's customers—which has the greatest impact on the bottom line.

ASK ABOUT STORIES

As a manager, use some of the time you waste talking about numbers to ask your salespeople to share stories about their clients and their clients' customers. In addition, listen to them and give suggestions for creative discovery. Ask how they would articulate the value from their client's customers' point of view.

That gives both parties a more realistic view of what the pipeline and forecast actually may be. By focusing the conversation on creative ways to get close to the client, pressure eases from both sides and deals get bigger.

Not only will this approach get you more sales, but it's more fun for everybody.

Another benefit for you as a manager is that hearing your sales reps tell stories allows you to know when they're onto something. You know when they're doing well and getting close. The more you know the story, the less pressure on both of you.

On Wallace's sheet, it's clear that this line of thinking and selling reduces the number of client touches it takes to get a response of any kind. Not only is Wallace signing more deals, but he's also signing them faster. And even if he does get a no, he gets it faster, too, meaning he can move on, making better use of his time.

DAVID LEWIS, VICE PRESIDENT ENTERPRISE ACCOUNT MANAGEMENT, ELLIE MAE, ON MANAGING BY DESIGN

My employee Sue (an account manager on David's team) has always been good at asking questions and being curious, but now she's so much more conscious of it. She said this put her discovery on steroids, to dive deeper. She just closed a $300,000 deal with one of our biggest customers. More importantly, we'll be shocked if they don't sign up for more services down the road. She has such a deep understanding of the customer's wants/needs that it's inevitable. The reason? Sell by Design taught her to spend more time in discovery, and she held back her first idea for a pitch.

With my entire team, there's a deeper level of engagement in how they share their stories. Our weekly one-on-ones have more depth. They're having deeper engagement with their customers overall.

We recently spoke with two customers, and they told us they noticed a real difference in our behavior. One told us she was under a lot of pressure implementing our system, and her rep, Kelly, has been incredibly helpful.

"She constantly checks in on how she's doing as a rep and how she can help. She wasn't there to sell me. She was genuinely interested in how I was doing, and how she could help get the system going and services she could help with. That wasn't the engagement I had with Kelly the first few months. It was more about 'When are you planning to launch? What kind of SVC do you need?'—very tactical. I can tell the difference now. I can tell that Kelly is genuinely interested in our success."

As a manager, I'm trying to reinforce this. I have them tell me the *why* and share personal stories about their accounts. I can read their account notes on my own. I want to hear a story about each of their customers so I know what's important to them. Hopefully, the habit will stick.

I don't point to their numbers because we all have numbers and dashboards in our faces all day long. It's deflating, and we all know the numbers anyway. I focus on helping them generate new ideas.

People think there's something wrong with being in sales, but Sell by Design proves salespeople can be genuine *and* successful.

HOW MUCH CAN YOUR CULTURE REALLY CHANGE?

At the conclusion of a recent Sell by Design workshop, a Salesforce executive told the team, "I'm not worried about your numbers." There was an unmistakable pause and silence in the room as people looked around at one another with something between smiles and expressions of disbelief. We knew we were getting somewhere.

He acknowledged the drumbeat and pressure of quota and pipeline and numbers, but at the same time, he knows that narrow focus is restricting them from bigger, missed opportunities. By focusing on people first and numbers second, both improve.

The cultural shift may be eventually drastic, but you can and should start small. Start with the low-hanging fruit. Where is there potential on the table? Where can you make some impact that others will see and begin to pay attention to? For Salesforce and Ellie Mae, the groundswell started with enterprise account reps because of their visibility in the company and the complexity of the accounts they manage. It could be the same or different in your organization.

Make time for this approach within your teams; it will get you better deals, it's more fun, and it provides you with stories to tell within your organization, shaping your culture and influencing future customers.

That's why the aforementioned Salesforce executive gave his people an unprecedented pass on their pipeline and quota for three months. It paid off with more than 100-percent gains in pipeline and in contract value for their targeted accounts.

It wasn't that he didn't *care* about the numbers; he just

wasn't *worried*. His people were doing good work, and they were going to hit their numbers without the mutually annoying hounding.

It all goes back to the model of desirability, feasibility, and viability. Feasibility and viability can't be ignored; you're in business to make money after all, but if you can't speak to desirability—what clients care about with an authentic point of view—you're at a competitive disadvantage. As a sales manager, there's a big payoff to be had by focusing on what's desirable and interesting to your sales teams and their clients.

We don't need to convince you that numbers matter. We do want to hammer home that these other things matter even more because they're ultimately what drive the numbers. Just as we've cautioned the salesperson in this book, don't let numbers be your Achilles' heel as the sales manager.

You're not just competing on the merits of your solutions; you're also competing as a trusted adviser in the co-creation economy. Whoever connects best will win.

We want you and your team to win big.

ABOUT THE AUTHORS

ASHLEY WELCH cofounded Somersault Innovation, a Design Thinking consulting firm providing a unique approach to sales development. Prior to Somersault Innovation, she spent twenty years as a leading sales professional for a leadership development company. She also founded TEDxYouth@Wayland. Ashley lives outside of Boston with her family.

JUSTIN JONES began his career in marketing and sales before moving into management consulting, innovation, and design. He has helped hundreds of teams apply design thinking against their toughest challenges and achieve breakthroughs. As cofounder of Somersault Innovation, he loves design's ability to surprise people with unexpected results. Justin lives in Denver with his family.

Made in the USA
Monee, IL
06 September 2021

76507820R10075